Urban Fishing in Toronto

A practical guide to fishing the Toronto shoreline

Mike Harry

First printing: 2014
Published by Interactive Hardware.
ISBN: 978-0-9937694-0-5

Urban Fishing in Toronto
By Mike Harry

Contact: www.fishingtoronto.com
admin@fishingtoronto.com

Ordering Information:
Special discounts are available on quantity purchases by corporations, sports associations and others. For details, contact the publisher at admin@fishingtoronto.com

Table of Contents

Urban Fishing in Downtown Toronto.................. 1

Basic equipment........................... 5

Toronto shoreline starting locations................ 9

Ashbridges Bay Park......................... 10

Tommy Thompson Park (TTP)..................... 16
    TTP the Bays............................ 20
    TTP the cells........................... 24
    TTP East Cove.......................... 26

Outer Harbour - Unwin Avenue.................... 28

The lower Don............................. 30
Toronto Islands Park......................... 32
    Wards – Eastern Gap..................... 34
    Sunfish Cut............................ 36
    Algonquin Island........................ 37
    The Boardwalk......................... 38
    Lookout Pier........................... 38
    St. Andrews Dock....................... 40
    Olympic Island Canal..................... 42
    Swan Pond............................ 45
    White Bridge........................... 47
    Grandstand............................ 48
    Old Trout Pond......................... 49
    Lighthouse Pond........................ 50
    Blockhouse Bay......................... 51

Hanlans Point.................................... 53

Harbour Square Park............................ 54

Coronation Park................................. 56

Ontario Place East.............................. 58

Ontario Place West............................. 60

Grenadier Pond................................. 62

Humber River Mouth........................... 63

Humber River Marsh........................... 65

Seasonal Species Notes....................... 67
    Early Pike – Dead Bait......................... 68
    Peak Pike Window.............................. 70

Bass Nights...................................... 72
    Blockhouse Bass.............................. 74

Toronto Carp 75
    The Hair Rig.................................... 79
    Carp Bait....................................... 83

Toronto Salmon Run............................ 85
    Downtown Salmon............................. 87

Rigs, Worms and Cranks....................... 89

Rigging Plastics................................. 90

Texas Rig.. 90

Carolina Rig...................................... 92

Wacky Rig... 93

Shaky Head...................................... 95

The Drop Shot Rig............................ 96

Crankbaits 101................................. 102

Lipless.. 103

Lip size and angle.......................... 106

Jointed cranks................................. 113

Useful Websites................................ 116

Author... 118

This page intentionally left blank

Introduction: Urban fishing in Downtown Toronto

In a country famous for its lakes, rivers and coastal waters, skyscraper studded downtown Toronto might not spring to mind as a prime location for shoreline fishing. In decades past, Toronto's Lake Ontario waterfront had been blighted by industrial wastelands, and an apparent lack of cohesive resource management. But, like the rest of this 21st century mega-city, the Toronto Harbour and waterfront has seen a recent boom in development, conservation and recreational access.

The City of Toronto, Waterfront Toronto and the Toronto and Region Conservation Authority have all been busy, moving forward with coordinated projects to re-vitalize the Toronto Harbour and waterfront area. Recent legislation and ongoing infrastructure projects have addressed the quality of the water, implemented new fish habitats, and developed protected wetlands to serve as fish spawning areas. The return of habitat sensitive baitfish, along with predators such as Bass, Pike and Walleye, signal that the recovery is well underway.

Once you know where to start, you will discover that the Toronto waterfront offers some of the best urban fishing experiences you will find anywhere. The diversity of the Toronto shoreline provides a range of fishing opportunities that can satisfy everyone, from the avid angler to the curious novice, or busy family. Some locations are perfect for a kid friendly pan fish expedition. Some for after work fishing sessions, straight from the office, and others offer spectacular night fishing.

This book covers locations specifically within the Toronto waterfront area, from Ashbridges Bay Park on the Scarborough border in the east, across downtown to the mouth of the Humber, at the Etobicoke border in the West. All locations can be easily reached via public transport. Detailed coverage is given in particular to the Toronto Islands and Tommy Thompson Park, as they both hold numerous sub-locations, and have generated the most questions by far, on where to start fishing.

The guide notes in this book are based on my personal fishing experiences along the Toronto shoreline since 2004. The starting locations listed do not represent anything like a complete list of fishing locations available on the Toronto waterfront.

You should bear in mind that fish habitat and other variables change season to season, and year to year. Be prepared to adapt accordingly, apply common fishing variables to the notes in this guide, such as how the water temperature, wind direction and time of day are applicable to your target species.

The onset of the inshore, summer fishing season, is primarily defined by the formation of warmer, thermal stratification layers across the top of Lake Ontario. This can occur anywhere between late May and early July, once the inshore surface waters climb above 4 degrees. Timing of this event varies from year to year, subject in large part, to the severity of the previous winter. Sometime around October, the falling autumn temperatures bring the surface waters back down below 4 degrees and the inshore water returns to its winter state.

The wide ranging temperature swing of the Toronto waterfront can present challenges if you set out to locate a particular species inshore, at what basically is the wrong time of year for those fish. However, as the lake holds both warm water and cold water species, it can also present the opportunity to 'go with the flow', if you are prepared to adapt to the lake's cyclic nature, and to target the fish species currently in residence.

No license – No fishing.

Almost everyone requires a license to fish in Toronto. Refer to the Ministry of Natural Resources website http://www.mnr.gov.on.ca/en/ for details on license requirements, the dates of closed seasons and the species restrictions, applicable to fishing in the Toronto area, BEFORE you start fishing.

Go to the fishing sub heading at the MNR site. You will find the license information and regulations under the 'getting started' heading. Download the zone map PDF to confirm which zone you are fishing in, and then locate the appropriate regulations document for that zone.

My annual fishing calendar usually runs something like this....

- Ice out in the shallow bays, and the pre-spawn winter pike are in Tommy Thompson Park, along the harbourfront walls and cruising the Toronto Islands lagoons.
- May, and the waters are warming up. The big carp are arriving in numbers into the harbour and Toronto Islands.
- End of June opens the bass season!
- Summer brings the pan fish and perch into the Islands, Ontario Place and the Marinas.
- September, and the falling temperatures and rains bring the salmon runs into the river mouths across Toronto.
- Late September, early October brings big brown trout into Ashbridges bay and the Humber marshes.
- October through to ice up, the big pike are back, and trout are in the local rivers.

Basic Equipment

On the one hand, it seems that you can never have enough fishing rods and reels, types of lures, tackle boxes and new gadgets. But on the other hand, you can be very successful with just a selection of basic items if you choose wisely, and carry the appropriate items for the fishing situation at hand.

I have put together my own basics list, comprised of the items that I think I could get by with in Toronto, over the course of an entire fishing year. Use my list as a reference for fishing the waterfront, and prioritise the equipment that you really need, to create your own list.

Seven foot spinning rod - Medium power, marked as suitable for line rated between 4 to12lbs, and lures of 1/8 to 3/4 oz. My "everyday" fishing rod used for most sight fishing expeditions.

Medium spinning reel - A wide spool spinning reel optimum rated for 120yds of 8lb line. It comes with two spools, I carry both. One spooled with 8lb fluorocarbon, and the other with 8lb braid.

Twelve foot casting rod - A longer, heavier rod capable of tackling large carp at distance, or salmon inside east cove is a must. Heavy power, marked as suitable for line rated between 12 to 25lbs, and a max lure weight of 4ozs

Big spool spinning reel - Long spool spinning reel for distance casting, optimum rated for 250yds of 20lb line.

Multi-pocket backpack - A small backpack with lots of pockets on the outside. This puts a practical limit on the amount of stuff that I can haul around on a day trek across the Toronto islands.

Plastic storage boxes - At the minimum, I would expect to carry at least four, clip-down lid, plastic storage boxes.

- one box of weights and split shot
- one box of hooks, swivels and beads
- one box of crankbaits and spinners
- one box of plastics and swimbaits etc.

Bait bag - A washable, foil lined, zip up bait bag designed for carrying packs of bait.

Tools - A selection of useful items.

- Metal water bottle.
- A small multi-tool Leatherman.
- A pair of thin, long nose pliers for deep hooks.
- A pair of wire cutters for cutting hooks.
- Two flashlights, one clip on, one normal.
- A small first aid pack.
- A whistle.
- A hand cloth.
- Cellphone.

A spare spool of fishing line - Useful for making up new rigs and traces while you are fishing, or replacing leaders without stripping line from your reel.

Landing net or drop net - A wide mouth, folding landing net, or a drop net for higher locations, is a must for safely landing fish at many of the waterfront locations.

Polarised sunglasses - A must have item with so many sight fishing locations available. Polarised sunglasses will give you a significant advantage.

You could easily add another hundred items if you took the list down to the detail level, naming specific types of lures, or itemising "a reel of spider wire" etc. This is a basic shortlist, aimed at general fishing of the species you are likely to encounter along the Toronto waterfront.

Obviously, you wouldn't need to carry multiple rods and reels for an after work fishing session on the boardwalk, at Harbourfront Park in July. But, you would be foolish to head down to East Cove on a Sunday morning without drinking water, a first aid kit, a cell phone and a whistle.

If you decide at some point to concentrate on a single species, then your fishing tackle will become more specific in nature. It's not uncommon to end up with multiple set ups, aimed at specific species, that come out for a month or two each year, with a general use rod and reel, filling the gaps.

Here's a quick run-down of the various setups that I have acquired in recent years.

- Seven foot "everyday use" medium spinning rod.
- Twelve foot heavy carp rod.
- Nine foot heavy spinning rod for pike.
- Six foot, light tackle spinning rod for pan fish and perch.
- Nine foot heavy travel rod.
- Six foot light tackle travel rod.
- Twelve foot medium-light Interline rod for weed plunking bass and drifting for trout.
- Eighteen foot beach caster for night fishing salmon, carp and Gaasyendietha.

Once you start to focus on a specific species as your primary fishing target, you will undoubtedly accumulate secondary items that are of no use in targeting other species.

For example, my rod tripods, electronic bite alarm and Chair-Pak are great for carp and night fishing sessions, but are no use at all for tracking through the bushes, sight fishing.

Plan ahead, check the weather, temperature and water conditions, pick your location and target species, then select and pack your kit.

Toronto Shoreline Starter Locations

Ashbridges Bay Park

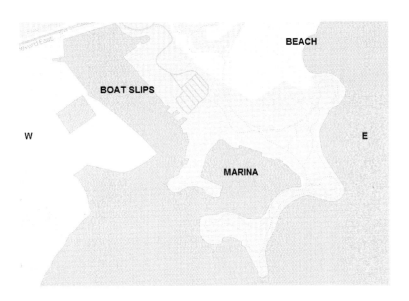

The road entrance to Ashbridges Bay Park is located on the east side of Toronto, south of the junction at Lakeshore Boulevard and Coxwell Avenue. (43.662288, -79.314863)

The park has a good amount of public parking available, and can also be easily reached on public transport. It's a 15 minute walk south on Coxwell from the Queen east and Coxwell TTC stop. The park is large, family friendly and best known for its long, wide beach.

There's a great boardwalk in Ashbridges Bay Park which runs along the Martin Goodman trail around the south peninsula of the yacht club marina.

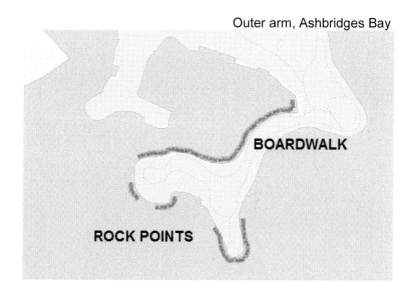

Outer arm, Ashbridges Bay

BOARDWALK

ROCK POINTS

If the ice in the bay has gone in late February or early March, you can target the pike using dead bait before the season closes. If we have had a hard winter with ice remaining through April, you still have a good shot at larger pike being around the bay when the pike season re-opens.

Static dead bait, or jointed crankbaits fished low and slow, are the best options immediately after season opener.

Drop shot fishing from the edge of the boardwalk at Ashbridges Bay for perch and pan fish with the kids can be very productive during the summer, use small hooks tipped with pieces of live worm.

Perch

Summer fishing for other species can be hit and miss during the main part of the day, possibly due to the amount of noisy boat traffic traversing the small bay. Early mornings, and either side of sunset when the traffic dies down, can be productive, especially if the bay is windward of an easterly breeze.

Mid to end of September through October is usually the time to start fishing for the big brown trout that have been regular catches at Ashbridges Bay over the last few years.

Brown Trout

The shallow end of the bay near the road entrance to the park is much quieter then the main bay, and provides trout with a lot of cover during the day.

There is little to no current in this end of the bay, so go with casting and retrieving bright spoons or trout worms. At night when the brown trout are more actively feeding, set up on the far end of the boardwalk, or the rock points on the outside of the park. Use a longer rod if possible, and cast farther out, for trout feeding at the entrance to the bay.

From May onwards there's also carp action to be had at Ashbridges Bay. Both in the main bay, and up in the shallows near the park entrance.

Back of the inlet, Ashbridges Bay

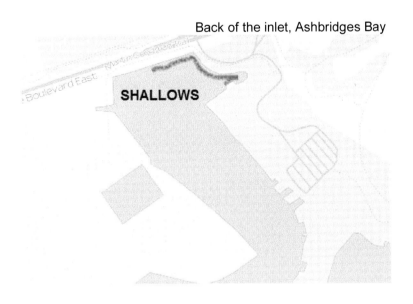

Keep the equipment simple for when you are edging through the bushes. Wear dark clothing and keep a low profile, the fish can see you just as well as you can see them.

Once bass season opens, this end of the inlet can still hold bass in the weed beds. Plunking a worm into the gaps as you quietly work your way around the edge can produce a nice surprise. I have also taken one or two catfish in the shallows here, using fresh worms.

Carp can usually be sight fished on hair-rigged pieces of corn or bread among the weeds in the shallows. I have also had a lot of success here using red kidney beans for carp. I don't know if the carp mistake them for beetles when they hit the water, or if they just like kidney beans.

Ashbridges Bay Park Boardwalk is one of the most kid friendly of the Toronto fishing spots. Easy access to the park for an hours drop shot fishing for perch and pan fish with the kids, right next to a big beach, and a great spot for a BBQ.

CAUTION: I strongly recommend that you use extreme caution, and go with a friend when fishing anywhere near the outside rock points of Ashbridges Bay Park, day or night. The ground is rough, and while with care it is possible to find a solid rock outcrop to cast from, it is also very easy to take a simple misstep and trip, or to fall from the rocks. Unlike the boardwalk, the rock outcrops are not a kid friendly fishing location.

Tommy Thompson Park (TTP) is located at the foot of Leslie Street where it meets Unwin Avenue, south of Lakeshore Boulevard East. (43.652362, -79.322936) The park is only open to the public on weekends and holidays year-round, (closed on Christmas Day, Boxing Day and New Year's Day). Operating hours are from 9am to 6pm March to November, and 9am to 4:30pm November to March. Opening hours are likely to change, to include week days, once the park is completed. Admission and limited parking are free. There is a TTC bus route that travels down Leslie as far as Carlaw, from where it's a 10 minute walk down to the Park entrance.

Tommy Thompson Park is a completely man made landfill site. It was started around 1959 as a drop site for harbour dredging, excavation and demolition rubble, and it now extends more than 5 km's out along the coast of Lake Ontario.

One of the effects of Tommy Thompson Park extending so far out into Lake Ontario is that the Toronto Islands no longer stand in the sand flow from the Scarborough Bluffs. Without the existing Island breakwall, shoreline structures and trees holding it together, the Toronto Islands would slowly be reclaimed by Lake Ontario.

TTP is so much more than just another city park, it's an urban wilderness, and one of its main objectives is to provide critical habitat areas for wildlife along the waterfront. In addition to the more than 300 species of birds that have been documented at TTP, the park is home to many mammals including Coyotes, which have successfully denned in the park for many years, and are observed on a regular basis.

NOTE: It's a 5km walk from the entry gate to the lighthouse at the other end of the park.

- No pets are allowed in the park.
- No vehicles are allowed in the park.
- There is a ban on live fishing bait (Worms are ok).
- Provincial fishing licences are required.

Stay alert as you walk through the park, it is very popular with cyclists, some of whom travel at extreme speeds along the pathways.

Native fish habitat enhancement projects are still ongoing within the park. Completed projects have already improved conditions for fish within the bays, including successful pike spawning in the cut channels.

According to the MNR and recent fish surveys taken at TTP, here are the most common fish you will find at the park, subject to the water temperature changes throughout the year.

- Northern Pike
- Largemouth Bass
- Yellow Perch
- Black Crappie
- Freshwater Drum
- Brown Bullhead

- Lake Trout
- Common carp (listed as invasive species)
- Walleye (being restocked along waterfront)

If you are wondering what natural colours of plastics or crankbaits match the forage fish located in the waters of TTP, here's the list of the most common prey fish found at the park, during various times of the year.

- Alewife
- Rainbow Smelt
- Emerald Shiner
- Spottail Shiner
- Bluntnose Minnow
- Round goby – (listed as invasive species)

Please remember that Tommy Thompson Park is a unique location to fish, and treat it with the utmost respect. Do not leave anything behind, especially hooks or discarded lengths of fishing line that could harm the birds or wildlife in the park. Some woodland areas surrounding the western bays are clearly marked as no entry between April and September, due to nesting birds. Please obey all the posted signs and stick to the marked paths when travelling between fishing locations.

Tommy Thompson Park

OUTER HARBOUR

CHERRY ST BEACH

BAYS C, D

MARINA

CELLS 1,2,3

BAYS A, B

SHIPWRECK

LIGHTHOUSE

There are four bays that face toward the outer harbour and the Toronto Islands side of Tommy Thompson Park. Three are shallow water bays and one is divided between shallow habitat, and the deeper marina area of the Aquatic Park Sailing Club. The fish habitat construction work performed on the bays has been extensive, and is still ongoing.

Embayment A

Bay A has received significant shoreline habitat development, and has been enhanced with backwater lagoons, spawning channels, rock shoals and log habitat piles.

Embayment B

Bay B has been extensively modified with the addition of strategically placed structures, in order to form various types of fish habitat. Rock shoals, underwater brush, dead trees and stumps have been placed in both the shallow and deep areas. Submerged log cribs filled with rubble have been submerged within the protected portion of the bay, and provide additional shelter for warm water species including bass and perch.

One of the more major structural modifications to bay B is the artificial barrier across the back end of the bay. This provides protection from wind and wave action as well as thermal protection from the colder waters of the main Lake Ontario. Shallow pike spawning channels have been cut into the edges of bay B.

During the mid - 90's fish surveys found Bass, Pike, Salmon, Perch and a variety of forage species in the immediate vicinity of bay B. In addition, adult northern pike were identified as spawning in the pike channels.

While most of the modifications to the fish habitat in Tommy Thompson Park overall are aimed at reducing the impact of carp to the benefit of other species, there are still trophy sized carp to be had in these bays. In particular, you can sight fish decent sized carp in bay B. It is also possible to target the largest of Toronto's carp population (40lb+) by casting offshore at this location.

Embayment C

Bay C is a sheltered warm water area created in 1975 and developed through modification of the shoreline structure, and the addition of wetland vegetation. The west side of the bay C deep cove, is a cool water fish habitat. The placement of structural habitats of the type outlined in bay B, have also been constructed in bay C.

Northern pike spawning channels were created along the eastern shoreline of bay C, just north of the channel into Cell 3. Pike have been observed successfully spawning in the channels.

Areas of gravel bed were added into bay C, in order to diversify bottom types and create Bass spawning habitat. Large pieces of stone were also strategically placed within the basin to create underwater reefs.

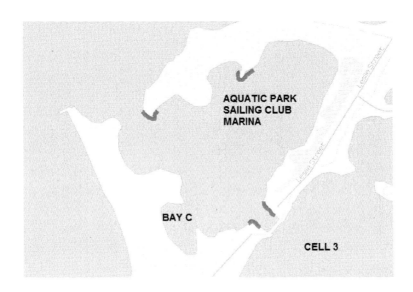

If you take the signposted Aquatic Park Sailing Club side road, from the main Leslie street path inside Tommy Thompson Park, it is possible to continue past the boat house, and onto a footpath that will lead you around the edge of the peninsula behind it. There are several fishable openings along the path, both on the inside, facing the marina bay and the outside, facing Cherry beach.

Overall, this can be a very productive area. The marina and bay C areas are prime pike fishing grounds. The flats outside the bay heading into the outer harbor area hold groups of large carp.

Either side of the footbridge that separates the inside of Bay C from Cell 3 is a high traffic point for fish entering and leaving the cells.

Bay C and the trench on the outer, western side of Tommy Thompson Park are known pike wintering grounds.

Embayment D
The west side of bay D is an enhanced fish habitat shoreline. Further enhancements scheduled for bay D will focus improvements on warm water fish habitat as previously performed in the Cell One Wetland. Access is restricted during construction.

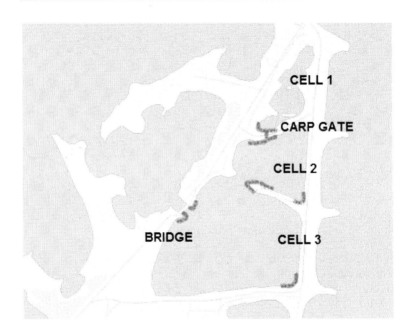

The inner cells of Tommy Thompson Park are under development into wetland areas. Cell one has been completed, Cell two is scheduled for 2014 / 15, cell three to follow.

Cell 1

Cell 1 has been fully developed as a wetland area and is now separated from Cell 2 by a carp gate installed across the Cell 1 entrance point. This has successfully prevented large adult carp from entering the wetland and destroying the plants. Significant numbers of carp can be seen just outside the carp gate from around June onwards. There are a number of fish species now successfully spawning in Cell one.

Cells Two and Three

Cells Two and Three currently have mixed fish communities, and habitat enhancements are ongoing. Cell 2 is designated for capping and restructuring as wetland habitat during 2014/15. Cell 3 is a prime winter holding location for largemouth bass and carp.

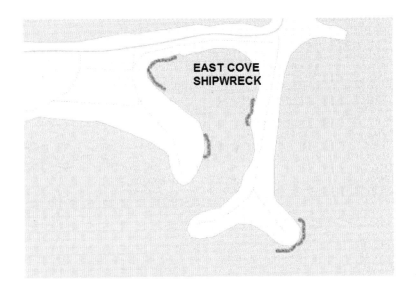

East Cove is a deep water inlet located at the far end of the park, to the east of lighthouse point. At its centre, East Cove is almost 40 feet deep with steep sides and large rock formations on the bed. There's a shallow area with a coarse pebble beach at the closed end of the curved inlet. The cove is well suited for cold water fish and aside from the large boulders; east cove holds another hidden and significant fish habitat structure. The 90ft long, 1920's lake cruiser "Southern Trail" lays scuppered in this cove. The largely intact remains of the boat are sitting upright on the cove floor, and its flat roof has partially detached, hanging to one side. This is an occasional, day time dive spot in the summer months, so be aware of boats and dive flags.

You can encounter trophy sized pike in this cove year round, as well as large brown trout and salmon in the autumn. Make sure you have the correct equipment for tackling these fish, lightweight spinning setups will not perform well in a fight with fish of this calibre, down among the boulders and structures that this cove holds. Both east cove and the nearby lighthouse point are excellent salmon fishing spots during the annual runs.

CAUTION: I strongly recommend that you use extreme caution and go with a friend when fishing the shoreline at the far end of Tommy Thompson Park. The ground is very rough here, and only with extreme care is it possible to access the beach, shoreline, or find a solid rock platform to cast from. It is very easy to take a simple misstep and fall from the rocks or to trip on the lengths of rusty rebar that protrude from the ground.

This section of the park is not a kid friendly fishing location.

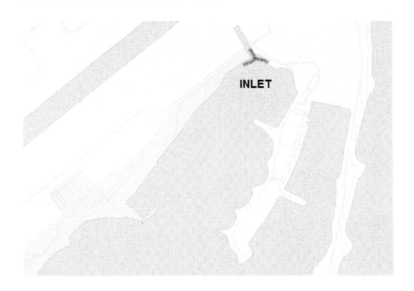

The far end of the Toronto Outer Harbour, on the Cherry Beach side can be accessed from Unwin Avenue (43.648150, -79.328621). It is possible to park at Cherry Beach and walk 15 minutes along the shoreline path. You can also park east of the inlet, further along on Unwin Avenue for a marginally shorter walk. There is seasonal public transport available as far as the Cherry Beach turning circle.

There is a power station exhaust water channel on Unwin Avenue at the far end of the Cherry Beach shoreline. The warmer water and sometimes fast flow attracts fish year round. You can sight fish either side of the mouth of the inlet, on the outside of the bridges. You can also access the nearby gravel beach down at water level, if you want to set up just outside the channel, and target the fish as they are entering and exiting. Do not attempt to access the railing area further up inside the channel, as the channel beyond the bridges is located on private property.

The open water area from cherry beach up to the inlet is relatively shallow with a sandy bottom on the Cherry Beach side. There is a deeper trench running down the opposite side, closer to the outer harbour marina peninsula. The waters in this area tend to warm earlier than most. Decent sized carp have been caught here, year round. Both Unwin Inlet and the outer harbour trench are significant wintering areas for carp and pike. The Unwin Avenue inlet is one of the few year round open water fishing locations due to the water temperature keeping the inlet ice free.

NOTE: It is also possible to fish the area directly opposite Cherry Beach, from the outside edge of the peninsula behind the Aquatic Park Boat Club in Tommy Thompson Park.

Lower Don River

By the 1850s, the Lower Don river had become an industrial waterway. Petroleum storage tanks and meat processing plants had been constructed and in 1879, the Don Valley Brick Works opened. Within a few years, pollution from these factories and the rapidly growing city was turning the Lower Don into a toxic hazard.

In the 1880s, the lower part of the Don was straightened eastwards and diverted to create additional harbour space. Known as The Don Improvement, the river was reset to divert its polluted waters away from Toronto Harbour, and into the Ashbridges Bay marsh.

Gooderham and Worts also made extensive use of the marshlands to dispose of waste from pigs and cattle, as well as the wheat swill from their distilleries. By the 1890's, the combination of these factors had reduced water quality within the marsh to the point where the immediate threat of Cholera forced the city into action. The mouth of the Don River was re-routed yet again, this time to the west, into the new Keating Channel. The marshlands were drained and filled; creating the foundations of what would later become the Toronto Portlands industrial area.

Today, while the Don Valley industries and their toxic legacy are long gone, the Lower Don does still suffer from the effects of urban runoff, in particular from the Don Valley Parkway and the surrounding neighbourhoods.

Waterfront Toronto, the City of Toronto and the Toronto and Region Conservation Authority continue to work together to revitalize the mouth of the Don. The abandoned Brickworks Quarry has already been repurposed as an arts centre, and the original quarry pit is now a series of shallow, wetland ponds. Instead of contributing pollution, the brickworks now filter water back into the Don River.

The Keating Channel and adjacent industrial areas at the mouth of the Don are currently under review for a major redevelopment into a wetlands park, with the river being redirected once more, back into a natural park and wetlands setting.

Despite its appearance, the Lower Don does hold fish. There are the usual Carp and Pike, plus the Don also has its annual Salmon and Trout runs. Water conditions can be quite poor in the lower areas of the river. Fishing can still be productive slightly further up the river, inside Riverdale Park.

NOTE: I haven't included any Lower Don locations in the guide due to its current water conditions. Here's hoping that the Lower Don regeneration project goes ahead, and we have a Lower Don wetlands park to fish in very soon.

Toronto Islands Park

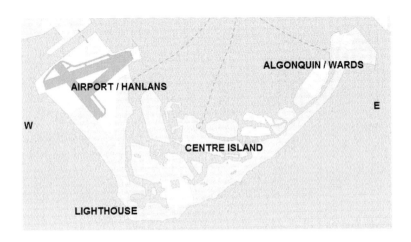

The Toronto Islands ferry terminal is located behind the Westin Harbour Castle hotel on Queens Quay (43.640279, -79.375019). There is a TTC station across the street from the Westin hotel that connects with union station.

Be aware that in winter, the ferry service runs to the Wards Island location only. The full service tourist ferry to Centre Island and Hanlans Point starts sometime around the May 24 holiday. Check with the ferry terminal or the website (see website index) for seasonal ferry schedules and fares.

The Toronto Islands have a wide range of seasonal fishing opportunities spread across an equally wide range of fish habitats. It may seem surprising at first that there are more fishing reports to be found online about getting skunked while fishing at the Islands, than there are reports of success.

To be fair, when asking about where to fish on the Toronto Islands most people are told "get the ferry to centre island, head to the white bridge and just start fishing", and obviously there's a bit more to it than that.

The time of day, the season, the amount of weed growth, oxygen levels, water temperatures and the current weather trend, are just a few additional factors that spring to mind before you even think about target species, presentation, tackle and bait etc.

Generally when you fish the Toronto Islands, the only thing for certain is that you are going to find yourself covering a lot of ground.

The Toronto Island locations in this section are set up in order from the Wards Island at the east end, across to the Hanlans point at the west. It's a 5km walk from Wards Island around to Hanlans Point, not including the side stops in and around Olympic Island.

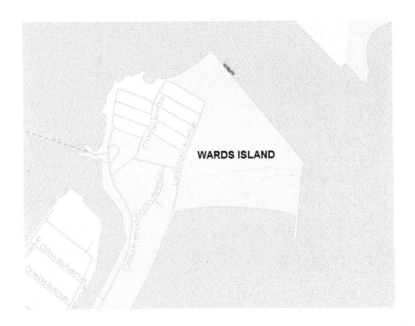

Walk straight ahead when leaving the Wards Island ferry dock. Head past the bowling green and the sport fields until you are in front of the public washrooms, then turn left onto Lakeshore Avenue (away from the boardwalk). Walk down to the end of Lakeshore Avenue and proceed onto the dirt track through the trees in front of you. You will emerge from the trees onto the concrete deck of the Eastern Gap.

The Eastern Gap is a man-made channel that averages 25ft deep and has good wall structure. The Wards Island side of the gap is hit with first light, and shaded by tall trees long before sunset, so the evening fish traffic rush hour, gets an early start here. I have had a lot of success with a wide range of species throughout the year at this location. Pike, Carp, Pan fish, Bass and Salmon all travel though this channel. Most travel close to the wall. Summer bass and carp can be sight fished, cruising along at around three feet below the surface.

Keeping it simple, float drifting a worm next to the wall, or walking the concrete deck and fan casting a small spinner parallel along the length of the wall has produced good results. Fishing the bottom with live bait will mostly yield bait stealing gobies by the bucket full. I recommend keeping the bait fishing relatively shallow, despite the available depth. Having said that, the soft mud bottom of the Eastern Gap can be fished close to the wall with a drop shot rig, goby-proof vertical jigging lures, or skirted Jig heads.

Algonquin Island, Sunfish Cut, the Boardwalk & Lookout Pier

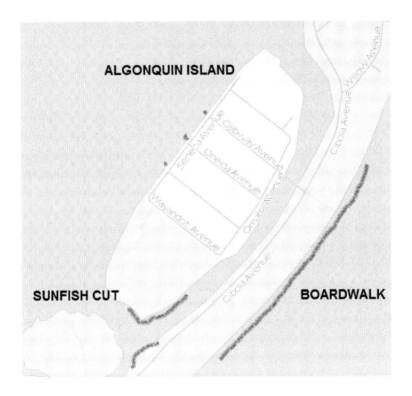

Sunfish Cut

One of the more popular fishing spots on the Toronto Islands is Sunfish cut. You can fish in the gaps between the bushes from the main path, for the resident pike using spinners or crankbaits.

However, a less crowded location is on the Algonquin Island side of the cut. Cross the large wooden bridge onto Algonquin Island and turn left to travel down Omaha Avenue to the end. Take the footpath straight on through the bushes past the little boathouses, until you emerge on the Sunfish Cut sand spit, at the corner of the island. You can fish the entire cut from here, fan casting around the peninsula. More often than not, you will have the entire beach section to yourself. It's a great spot to spend the afternoon. Early or late in the day, target the shadow line area between light and shade on the water.

Algonquin Island

Back up the trail a hundred yards or so, and you can sometimes spot large groups of carp in the canal once the summer weeds are in full flow. This section of the canal can't be seen or fished at all from the main road, due to the dense undergrowth. It can be effectively sight fished from the trail on the higher Algonquin Island side, or from down at water level on the narrow beach.

Take a walk around Algonquin Island, onto the Toronto inner harbour side, and you will see wooden picnic tables set along the front wall of the island. It's possible to fish the sand flats in front of Algonquin Island in the evenings for small harbour pike, through the openings in front of the picnic tables.

The Boardwalk

The Island's concrete breakwall along the boardwalk is protected with huge boulders along the outside. The boardwalk is one of the least fished locations on the islands, and with good reason. There is rarely any fish action here during the day.

However, at sunset in the summer, I have had success targeting smallmouth bass among the boulders outside the wall. A shallow running crankbait, or a top water lure after dark, played over the submerged boulders will bring them out of their hiding spots. Walk the length of the boardwalk to cover as much water as possible.

Lookout Pier

Without doubt the trophy for least fished, "but productive at the right time", spot on the Toronto Islands, is the lookout pier. I have never encountered another fisherman here in ten years of fishing. Again, during the day there is no action, unless you are balloon drift fishing the edge of the channel at distance. (A long story and not one for this book....)

After sunset, you can target pretty much every fish species that the island has to offer passing by, including salmon during the annual run. The pier head is fitted with street lights and just outside the borders of the light to dark transition area on the water seems to be the most productive. Deep-diving, jointed crankbaits work well at night, with little to no worry about snags, as the pier faces out onto the flat, open waters of the sand bar.

NOTE: A word of caution, the pier is at least fifteen feet above the water level, so I would highly recommend a drop net for hauling up the fish.

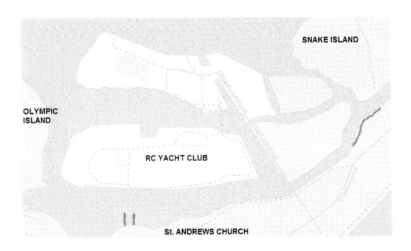

Tucked away on the other side of the bushes behind St. Andrews Church, situated across the canal from the Royal Canadian Yacht Club, are two long wooden docks. You can target schools of perch under the docks with worm pieces here in the summer. Take care if you are with kids, as the water is deeper than you might think. There are usually small pike waiting in ambush on the edges of the weed beds, further out in the junction. During the summer, bass can sometimes be found beneath the moored boats on the opposite side of the canal, if you have a long rod and the casting arm to reach them. If not, you can move east along the canal towards the RCYC bridge, where the canal narrows.

If you travel east past the Yacht club towards the snake island bridge, you can find early season bass and perch action in the junction just west of the bridge. The canal will increasingly fill with weeds as the summer builds, and it may prove difficult to access the shoreline at all if the bushes are having a high growth year. There are a lot of mussels beneath the waterline on the wooden structure of the bridge, which in turn draws swarms of gobies in the summer months. Be advised that live bait won't last long here under the goby onslaught

Olympic Island Canal

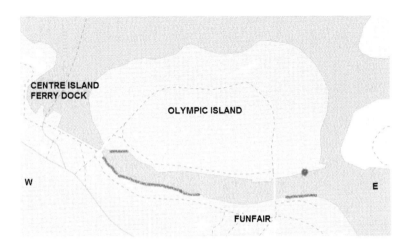

     This location is the closest one to the Centre Island Ferry dock. The Olympic Island canal is closed to boat traffic, enclosed within a low footbridge at either end. The area just inside the footbridge at the end nearest the funfair, has a section of the canal roped off for pedal boats, when the funfair is open. The area just inside the bridge at the end nearest the ferry dock, has significant sandbar build up under the bridge and into the canal, effectively making a dead end for all but the smallest of fish.

     Average depth of this canal varies between four to eight feet, sloping from the ferry dock end, down towards the funfair end. The ferry dock end of Olympic canal becomes completely weed blocked by mid-summer. The weed beds hold perch and bass, while carp regularly patrol up and down the canal from the funfair end bridge, to the sandbar and back.

Plunking earthworms into the weed beds can be very effective. Top water plugs over the top of the weeds are also good on early mornings and just after sunset. Be wary of trying to pull spinners through the heavy weeds.

Canned Corn

The carp in the canal respond well to corn kernels, red kidney beans, flavoured packbaits and boilies. Presentation can be hair rigged and offered as single items, enclosed with packbait or popped up off the bottom.

At the eastern end of Olympic Island, just beyond the blue pedestrian bridge there is a high wooden platform that protrudes out over the water, overlooking the canal junction. From here you can sight fish and target carp from May onwards as they move in and out of the shallows. You will need a long handled landing net, or a drop net to land the larger carp.

On the opposite shore from the old wooden dock, in front of the funfair, there is a docking position for the Island pontoon boat. From here you can also fish for the carp in the weeds at the canal junction, while down at water level. You will lack the overhead view of the Olympic Island platform, but it is much easier to land the fish.

Note: Be sure to keep well clear of the scale railway tracks that run along the edge of the canal in front of the funfair.

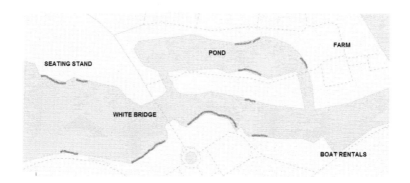

Swan Pond

The Swan Pond is located south of the funfair, and just west of Far Enough Farm. There's crazy carp action in the Swan Pond from May up to sometime in late summer, when the combination of extreme high water temps and low water levels, will take the oxygen level down too low, even for carp. Use corn kernels, cut worms or crusty bread, and sight fish with a stealthy approach. The majority of fish traffic at the pond is down towards the end where the farm is located, and around the tree islands in the main pond.

Do not fish from the small gauge railway bridge or across the tracks, there is a scale train that travels on a long loop from the funfair, round to the pond and back. The wagons are usually packed with kids, and the driver won't take kindly to having someone fishing from the bridge or railway tracks.

The inlet under the short bridge at the café end of the pond is sometimes blocked by a sand bar, so fish are usually only traveling in and out via the other end.

A hidden location near the pond can be found behind the large storage shed, just beyond the back of the restaurant. There's a sunken tree in the main canal (not the swan pond). Decent size carp can be found here resting under the trees in the summer. Keep a low profile and keep well back from the stone steps at the water's edge, when sight casting to these fish. Be prepared to move fast if one of these fish takes your bait and makes a run for the main canal.

The Swan pond is one of the best carp sight fishing opportunities you can get. Take a day off during the week and have the pond to yourself. If you are looking to try fly fishing for carp, the shallow waters of the Swan Pond are a great place to start.

The White Bridge

Walk straight on along the main path from the centre island ferry dock, and you will come to the spot most people are sent to if they ask about fishing on the Islands. "Take the Centre Island ferry, walk to the white bridge and start fishing". You can fish either side of the white bridge on its south shore. The east side is the canal in front of the Swan Pond Café where you can find pike under the bridge in the early season, and fairly large schools of perch in the canal from around June. West side of the bridge is Long Pond. On the south shore, the stone steps are in front of a deep hole, located in the centre of the canal.

Decent sized Pike can be caught in the deep zone in early spring and late autumn. Fishing tends to die off here during the day in the summer once the tourist boat traffic picks up. But early summer mornings and evenings around sunset can still produce a variety of fish.

The Grandstand

Get to the grandstand on the north shore of Long Pond in the early mornings before the boat traffic starts up and you can usually target carp patrolling in the main channel, as well as pike in the weeds. Targeting the pike will require you walking the shoreline alongside the bandstand, as the pike tend to hold ambush positions in the weeds rather than actively patrolling.

NOTE: Don't set yourself up for a long term carp session on the grandstand during the summer. Several of the tourist boats and water taxis regularly drop off passengers at this location. Also, be aware that the deep trench area out in the centre of the canal, in front of the grandstand, is where the large tourist boats make a U-turn on the mid-point of their route.

Old Trout Pond & Lighthouse Pond

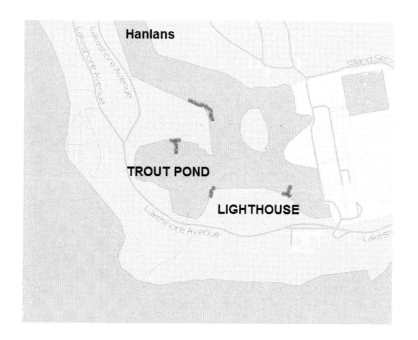

Trout Pond and Lighthouse Pond are situated south of Hanlans point at the Southwest tip of the Islands.

The old Trout Pond

To the best of my knowledge the Trout Pond is no longer stocked. I can state from experience however, that it does hold catfish under the lily pads in early summer.

There's a half sunken platform on the north side of the Trout Pond that you can access through the bushes behind the metal storage container. From here you can pitch a live or plastic worm into the lily pads and weed beds. You can also make your way around the south side of the pond past the bench, and fish the shallows, or head through the trees to the Trout Pond opening into Lighthouse Pond.

Lighthouse Pond

There is no public access to the east or north sides of Lighthouse pond. However, if you walk east along the shore behind the stone lighthouse, you should be able to spot a short floating dock that will allow you decent access at water level on the south side of the pond. The pond holds quite a few species and they largely go undisturbed, due to the difficult access.

Blockhouse Bay

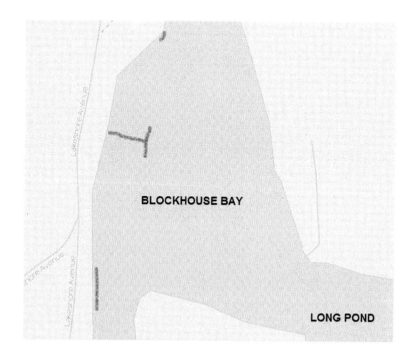

At the west end of Long Pond and south of Hanlan's point is Blockhouse Bay. This is a renowned pike hot spot. Early and late season you can take advantage of the empty floating dock on the west bank of the main canal and cast further out into the junction. Once boating season is in full swing is it difficult to access any decent shore spots here. Try to get in at the north and south choke points where the junction narrows back into the canals.

Blockhouse Bay is a significant winter holding location for largemouth bass. The far side of the canal just south of the Blockhouse Bay junction holds numerous pools and tree filled inlets under dense cover.

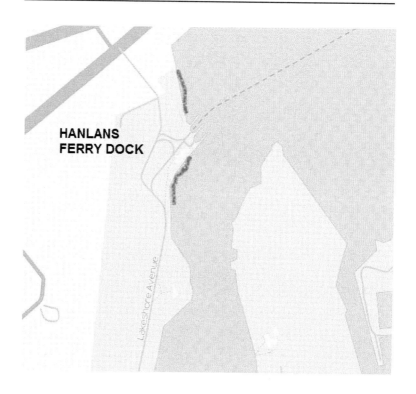

HANLANS
FERRY DOCK

The area just west of the Hanlans point ferry dock, toward the airport fence is fairly shallow, with a rocky bottom and good weed growth in summer. There's no boat traffic due to the proximity of the ferry dock on one side and the Airport exclusion zone on the other. A great summer's night fishing spot, lots of fish activity after dark, and a thirty second walk to catch the ferry.

NOTE: The Hanlans point ferry does not run year round, check with the ferry terminal or website for the current ferry schedule.

Harbour Square Park – Toronto Harbour

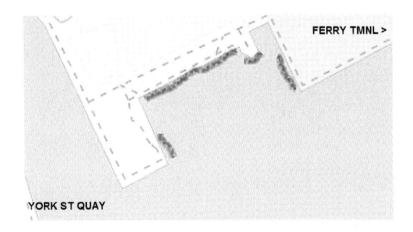

Harbour Square Park is located alongside the Toronto Island ferry terminal. (43.639377, -79.377106) The west side of the park, beyond the main park has a long section of boardwalk, set aside from the main shoreline path, down at the water's edge.

The water here is shallow and weedy with a waterfall situated in the park at the west side of the bay, and a high concrete lookout platform at the east side. This is a prime carp location for summer evenings and night fishing. Corn is the go to bait, but there is also the opportunity to sight fish from the lookout, by pitching live or plastic worms into the weeds.

June is the best month for pike fishing close to the waterfall. The high oxygenation, swirling eddies and good structure provides the perfect pike ambush point. Use spoons or pike streamers low in the water. You will need a drop net to land fish near the waterfall, unless you are able to cast out to the waterfall from the end of the boardwalk.

NOTE: Be aware that during the daytime in the summer there is a water taxi service operating from the Harbour Square boardwalk.

Do not fish from the outside wall of the west end of the park into the waters of York Quay, as York Quay is a high volume boat traffic area, and out of bounds.

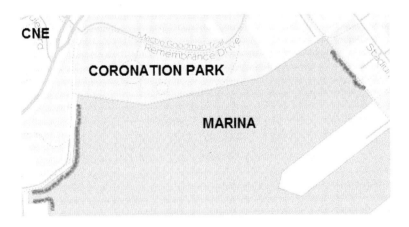

Located just outside the Western Gap of Toronto Harbour, and just east of Ontario Place is Alexandra Marina and Coronation Park. (43.633264, -79.405665) The Park can be reached via TTC service along Lakeshore to the CNE Prince's gate, which is across the street. The marina can be easily fished at either end, but there is a high metal rail along the length of the south shore of Coronation park, which makes landing large fish extremely difficult.

The sidewalk at the east end of the marina, behind HMCS York, offers good sight fishing for perch, pike and carp as well as the occasional roaming salmon. Walk the length of the wall, fan casting with small spinners or cut worms.

This is a great spot for pan fishing with the kids. There's lots of space on the wide sidewalk in front of the townhouses, and good line of sight into the water, allowing the kids to spot the fish.

The west end of the Marina, closest to Ontario Place has a stepped wall that runs around the end of the marina and into the shallow inlet. There is a variety of collapsed structure on the bottom at this end of the marina. You can find decent sized largemouth bass here once the season opens in June, providing that the water temperatures are up. You can also find pike in the tall weeds around the inlet at sunset. Smallmouth bass hide in the rocks at the very end of the inlet, and carp roam both ends of the marina in the evenings. In short, this end of the marina can be a very productive spot for a day's fishing, with a wide range of fish species available.

Stand on the outside jetty wall and cast spinners and crankbaits into the main lake, parallel to the Ontario Place shoreline, for a shot at the larger pike that lay in wait outside the marina entrance.

If you are targeting perch during the summer, move to whichever end of the Marina is downwind.

Ontario Place – East end

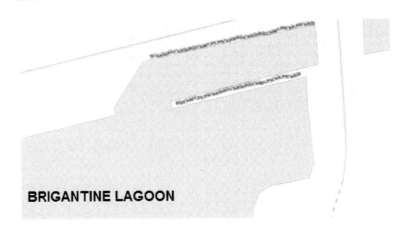

BRIGANTINE LAGOON

The area just inside the east end of Ontario Place, Next to Coronation Park is the Brigantine Lagoon, which is the closed end of the Ontario Place water system. (43.631001, -79.411025) The connector channel between OP and the Alexandra Marina is divided by the access road to the OP service car park. The end of the inlet is filled with rubble and houses a community of smallmouth bass. The deeper section of the inlet contains some large pieces of concrete rubble and provides significant cover for perch and pike. There is a stepped wall along the length of the inlet and a jetty wall that can be accessed to fish both the other side of the inlet, and the outside edge into the lagoon.

There is little to no boat traffic through this lagoon anymore, since the tourist boats are no longer allowed to launch from the private slip inside the OP service lot. The large ornate fountains located just under the surface in the centre of the lagoon, also no longer run, as Ontario Place is now closed.

58

The outside edge of the jetty wall, on the south side of the inlet, faces into the main lagoon. This location provides excellent late afternoon / early evening Carp fishing in the weeds throughout the late spring and early summer months.

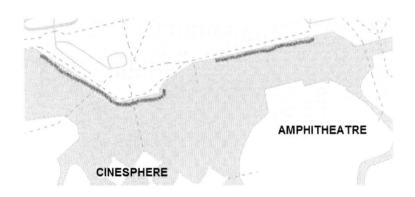

AMPHITHEATRE

CINESPHERE

Following the closure of the Ontario Place the northern shoreline that is accessible from public footpaths remains open for shore fishing. But only until such time as the site becomes a construction zone. The west end of the venue is where the tall white pillars support the high walkways across to the Cinesphere. (43.629577, -79.418351) It can be reached via TTC service to CNE, then walk across the CNE pedestrian bridge to Ontario Place.

This is a great pike venue, almost as good as Tommy Thompson Park, but much easier to access. Once the weed beds around the pillars have filled in, usually sometime around June, you can fish for trophy sized pike at this location. The wall edges and docks hold smaller pike year round, plus perch and the occasional bass. If the ice is out before the pike season closes, try dead bait for pike around the end of the docks.

The second location in front of the Molson Amphitheatre, is a narrow channel on the north side of the floating marina boat dock. Once the weeds fill in, and the water warms, you will find a decent amount of perch and pan fish in here, as well as the occasional carp patrolling the weeds.

A good location for targeting perch with the kids, I would recommend a drop shot rig to keep your bait off the bottom and away from the gobies, or float drift a live worm just across the tops of the weeds.

Grenadier Pond, High Park

Grenadier pond in High Park, Toronto suffered a huge increase in fishing pressure throughout 2012-2013. This was based on the rumours that fishing had been banned across the rest of the Toronto shoreline, (it's not) and that the Police marine unit were targeting any fishing activities on the waterfront.

As a result of the overfishing spike, there was also a marked increase in fishing related wildlife incidents at the pond. Grenadier pond has significant weed growth throughout the summer and birds were being killed or maimed by fishing hooks, lures and fishing line lost in the weeds, or carelessly dumped at the shoreline.

As of early 2014 there is a petition under review to ban fishing at Grenadier pond while a wildlife impact study is commissioned. It should be noted that the increased 2012 fishing pressure at the pond, and a mysterious "fish die off" event in 2013 has significantly depleted the fishing stocks.

Due to its current conditions and issues, Grenadier pond is not included in this book as a fishing venue.

Humber River Mouth

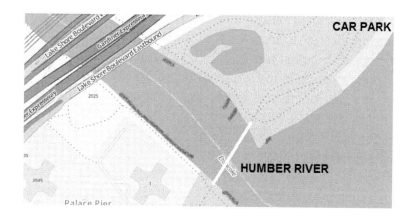

The mouth of the Humber River (43.632529, -79.471218) is located at the west end of the Lakeshore Boulevard Parklands. It can be reached on public transport if you take the TTC to the Humber Loop, and walk back across the bridge on Lakeshore. The mouth of the Humber holds pike and carp, pretty much year round. During the annual salmon run in September and October, it is possible to catch large salmon from the two low stone arms that protrude into the river, and from the rocks on the outside of the white arch bridge. Early mornings, and evenings after sunset are the best times of day for salmon, although when the run is at its peak, they can be caught during the daytime, especially if the day is overcast, or a day or two after heavy rainstorms.

Fish can also be taken from the rail on the opposite side of the river (next to the condo towers) but be wary of tackling any carp or salmon from here without a drop net to haul the fish up.

Large pike can usually be found slightly further up the river hiding in the dark waters, under the bridges, close to the supports.

The waters of the Humber rarely run anything like clear, and once the September rains start, they are as brown as chocolate milk. Go with the larger sizes of jointed crankbaits or glow spoons, for maximum effect when retrieved through the current. If you get upstream of the first set of bridges, you can drift the lures downstream close to the supports. I have had best results from targeting fish that were holding position in the back eddy behind the pillars.

Humber River Marsh

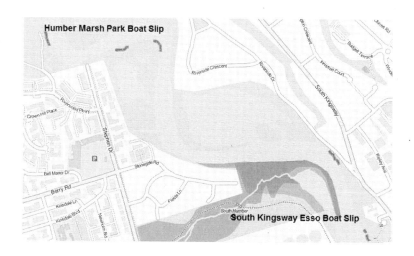

There are several good shoreline locations available, from which to take advantage of the fishing opportunities around the Lower Humber Marsh area. But it does involve a lot of walking through the bushes, and down dirt trails to get to the waters edge.

Starting on the Toronto side of the lower Humber, next to the Gas station on South Kingsway, there's a small public car park. (43.636093, -79.474947) Public transport runs just to the south along the Queensway, the closest TTC stop is Queensway at South Kingsway. Walk past the gate and down the long slip road. There's a public boat slip at the end of the path, and it is possible to fish the shoreline on either side. You can find decent size carp in the river here, although there are additional carp protection barriers going in all along the wetlands on the West side of the river.

Fishing for carp in the current at the boat slip will involve using a decent sized weight on your setup, in order to hold position on the river bed. Go with a longer rod and make sure that you have a lot of line on the reel. The carp at this location will run down river as soon as they get hooked.

Further up South Kingsway, just where it splits with Riverside Drive, there is a steep footpath beyond the rail that leads down to a small gravel spit on the inside of the river bend. (43.638261, -79.477470) You can fish for trout and pike, in the slower water along the front edge of the nearby reed beds here.

CAUTION: The footpath is steep and slippery, and the gravel beach does not exist during the spring run-off. Be aware that this is not a kid friendly fishing venue.

Further up river on the Etobicoke side, you can fish alongside the Humber Marsh Park public boat slip. (43.641831, -79.490631) You can fish for carp, trout and catfish in this section of the river. Casting upstream under the trees and float drifting a live worm back down in the current can produce results in the evenings. Walking the bank and plunking worms at the edge for catfish in the early mornings can also get results here.

It is possible to get down onto the wooded peninsula that extends eastwards out into the river, from the footpath at the very end of Stephen Drive. There are several shoreline locations on the peninsula once you get down to the water. This trek through the bushes, and is not suitable for after dark excursions.

Seasonal Species Notes

Pike

You don't have to limit your pike fishing technique to casting and retrieving spinners, spoons and crankbaits. Pike take a lot of winter kill from the shallows, and it's a good tactic before season close in the winter, and when the season first re-opens, to present dead bait as an easy meal.

There's nothing quite as frustrating as sight fishing a post-spawn pike right after the season opener in the Toronto Island canals. They can just sit there, motionless in the crystal clear water, watching your spinner or spoon, before casually turning around to face the other direction, totally disinterested.

A dead bait presentation can make the difference here, but even this technique can involve a lot of waiting. I waited for almost thirty minutes with the dead bait placed no more than twelve inches from the nose of a harbour pike, in clear water at Sunfish Cut. I was about to give up when he casually slid forward and slowly took up the bait.

Store bought jars of large Minnows, or bags of frozen Smelt have worked well for me in the past. Rig a treble hook through the back, with or without a stinger hook added to the tail. I would recommend using a short black wire leader, and wrapping the deadbait with some spider wire elastic thread to give the body a bit of a curve. Putting a curve into the bait is one of those tricks that developed over time, based on results. The tail or head sticking up slightly from the bottom seems to make the bait easier to spot, and for the pike to pick up. Don't expect a huge hit from the pike, 99% of my dead bait catches have been slow pick up, and turn-away pulls on the line. Don't forget that this is a stationary bait technique.

NOTE: Go with a decent size hook when dead baiting pike, avoiding the use of smaller hooks on dead baits will reduce the number of deep hooking incidents, and they are easier to grip and remove.

Pike on a lure

Once the spawning is over and the pike are rested, we move into prime pike season along the Toronto waterfront. It can vary slightly from year to year based on weather and temperatures, but overall the second half of May and the month of June produces serious pike action. Target the edges of tall weed beds and deep trenches, pike are expert ambush predators and prefer tall straight weeds over other types such as milfoil. My experience in locations such as Ontario Place and Alexandra Marina is that the pike will stage in the weeds, or among the large sunken boulders, facing out into deeper water.

Aside from the usual spinners, spoons and crankbaits, don't be afraid to try a pike streamer. I have found them very productive in the harbour, as you can get a decent rise and fall back motion that you won't get from a spinner.

If you are going pike fishing with spoons along the harbourfront, your preferred technique should be to go low and slow with your retrieves. Water depth here is an average of approximately fifteen feet, and the majority of the harbourfront pike are to be found lurking near the new habitat structures, right at the base of the walls.

Bass Nights

Largemouth Bass

Late summer, night fishing for bass on the Toronto Islands is largely overlooked by the majority of fishermen. The Island ferry service runs to around 11:30 pm throughout the summer, so getting there and back is not a problem. A couple of nights either side of a full moon have produced best results for me, especially if the night is clear. The moonlight produces a decent silhouette of the plug or crankbait moving through the water, when viewed from below by the fish.

The outside of the concrete breakwall on the south side of the islands provides both cover and food sources. Walk the boardwalk inside the wall and fan cast over the rock beds to draw out any bass that may be in hiding. The lookout pier also provides a good platform for night fishing this side of the islands. You can fish off the sides near the shore, just out past the beach breakwater wall, or head to the end of the pier to fish the sand bar. The lookout pier sits on the sand bar that is the foundation for the islands. Average water depth in front of the pier is around fifteen feet. Some way out from the pier, but still to this side of Tommy Thompson Park is a much deeper shipping channel that runs up the full length of the outside of the islands and turns left into the Eastern Gap, while also continuing straight on past the opposite shore from Cherry Beach. The channel holds fish during the day, and some move back into the shallows across the sandbar, after sunset.

In terms of set up, I usually rig a small swivel with an end clip, so that I can quickly change the type of lure that I'm using. Evening fishing on the boardwalk normally starts at the Ward Island end with a floating, shallow action crankbait. I make my way down the boardwalk towards the lookout pier, casting as I go. Once I reach the pier, I start using the shallow running crankbait off the sides of the inshore end of the pier, then move along to the head of the pier, beneath the street lights. Once you are at the end of the pier you can switch to a deeper running crankbait as the pier is located on a wide sand bar with little to no snags to worry about.

The return walk along the boardwalk from the pier back to the Ward Island ferry is normally much darker than the inbound trip, so I switch to a top water plug. Top water lures will give you a lot less hassle when fishing over the rocks outside the wall in the dark. They are easy to pause during a steady retrieve, and they make lots of fish attracting commotion.

NOTE: Be wary of using a live earthworm rigged under a float from the boardwalk after dark, you could find yourself hooked into a 20lb or 30lb carp with no way of getting it up the wall or pier, and out of the water.

If you want to target the large carp in this area at night, move up to the Ward Island Beach.

Blockhouse Bass

Another good spot for late summer night fishing for largemouth bass is at the opposite end of the Islands, south of Hanlans Point ferry dock. Head down the canal to the Blockhouse bay and Long Pond junction, there's a deep pocket in the centre of the junction that usually holds fish. The Hanlans canal just to the south of the junction holds several hidden inlets and tree filled basins amongst the bushes on the far side.

This is not a location that I have managed to fish every year, as sometimes there's so much boat traffic moored in the canal, it's not possible to get to the water's edge to fish.

This location is still worth visiting in October when all the boats have gone, as largemouth are known to winter at this location. Be aware that it's a long 5km walk around to the Ward Island ferry if the Hanlans Point summer service has ended.

Toronto Carp

Common Carp

If you haven't yet tried fishing for carp along the Toronto waterfront, then you are missing out big time. Carp are a powerful fish, fast growing, attaining maturity in around three years, but with a potential life span in excess of thirty years. The average weight for carp around the Toronto waterfront shallow areas is in the 10 to 20lb+ range. If you fish the Outer Harbour and Tommy Thompson Park, you could connect with carp in the 40lb+ range.

In defense of the bad-ass Carp

First, let's not confuse the naturalized Common Carp that lives along the Toronto Waterfront with the impending threat of the Asian Silver Carp, currently making its way up the Mississippi River, and towards the Great Lakes. It is not the same fish.

The Common Carp has had a long-term bad rep around Toronto, labelled as an invasive species almost one hundred and fifty years after being purposefully introduced as a food source in 1870.

The Common Carp has managed to survive a century of pollution in Lake Ontario without a stocking program, while many other fish species significantly faltered. Thankfully, today the waters of Lake Ontario along the Toronto shoreline are significantly cleaner. Numerous organisations, both government and privately funded are undertaking huge work projects to enhance the Toronto waterfront, and to develop the fish habitat. Toronto Island beach has regular blue flag status and the return of many bait fish and predators species to the inshore, is a good indicator of clean waters bringing the eco-system back to normal.

While there is no doubt that the unbalanced population numbers of carp impacts significant damage to plants in wetland areas, the notion that some anglers preach of carp being responsible for the decline of all other fish species, while ignoring the decades of urban and industrial pollution, is simply ridiculous.

The current measures to control the carp population in the Toronto area are focused on providing advantages to other fish species, by developing new wetland habitats and spawning grounds. These areas are then protected from carp related damage. Carp gates and other protective barriers are used to restrict carp access, moving toward rebalancing fish species populations, by significantly reducing the numbers of Common Carp spawning in the wetlands.

Euro style fishing for Toronto Carp?

Ontario's free ranging, world class, Common Carp fishery, has caught the attention of European fishermen in recent years. There is a booming, carp tourism fishery quickly developing, particularly along the Long Sault area of the St. Lawrence.

There are a few key differences between the style of carp fishing practised in Europe, and the options available for carp fishing in Toronto that you should be aware of before setting out.

Euro-Carp fishing tends to take place on stocked catch and release lakes, where the fish can become extremely wary of a particular bait or presentation. This has resulted in a huge industry dedicated to developing new baits, tackle and techniques, for use in attempting to catch the resident trophy carp, which has justifiably developed a keen sense of paranoia.

Carp fishing in Toronto can be considerably simpler. You still have the option for distance fishing a personal best trophy specimen in deeper waters, using specialised carp rigs and tackle, but you also have the option to sight fish for large carp in shallow waters, using only basic equipment.

Sight Fishing Toronto Carp

Let's start with the simpler option, sight fishing carp with a spinning rod and reel, a can of corn kernels and a pair of polarised sunglasses.

If you are sight fishing from the boardwalk at Harbourfront Park or the Swan Pond on Centre Island, you can fish effectively using a seven foot spinning rod. Obviously, you need a rod with sufficient backbone to tackle a 15lb+ fish, and your fishing reel must have a good drag system, with enough line to absorb a long carp run. Bait can be as simple as bread crust, but the most popular is a can of corn kernels. Throw a handful into the water and then cast your hook loaded with two or three kernels into the mix. It should be noted that Toronto waterfront carp will also take a cut worm or even a woolly fly. (Yes, you can fly fish for carp here too….)

Carp fishing with a Hair rig

Carp in the shallows will take insects, bread or berries off the surface, or even live worms suspended mid-water under a float. When they are actively feeding, carp primarily move around on the bottom, searching for small insects, crustaceans and plants. One of the probable reasons that there's such a wide range of carp baits, is that they will taste test pretty much anything once, to see if it's a viable food source.

Carp do have small teeth in the back of their throat for crushing insects and crustaceans, but no teeth in the front of their mouth for biting down on prey. The carp will draw in a mouthful of particles and then blow out again as it separates particles from food. The hair rig bait presentation is designed to take full advantage of this feeding method.

The hair rig bait presentation has emerged as the pre-dominant carp fishing rig, with numerous variations available. A basic hair rig comprises a short shank, wide gape hook usually around size 4 or 6, secured on a length of line terminating in a swivel. Above the swivel on your main line is where you place a sliding weight. This allows you to set a reasonably tight line against the weight and swivel, but allows the carp to draw the bait and line through the sliding weight without much resistance. The "hair" itself is a short length of line, ending in a small knotted loop, onto which you thread your bait and bait stop.

How it works

When the carp takes the bait in, the hook follows, and as the carp expels, the bait travels back down the hook shank, drawing the hook out point first across the carps lip. Round, wide gape hooks will give you a high rate of cleanly lip-hooked fish. One of the key elements of this basic rig is for the hair length to be more flexible than the hook length leader. This allows the slightly stiffer hook length to maintain the hook in the correct position, while the bait hair, being more flexible moves back easily across the hook shank. A simple solution for achieving this is to use braided line for the hair, and to gently scrape the hair length before use, removing the outer cover and making it more flexible than the hook length.

Carp fishing at distance

With the increasing popularity of carp fishing in Ontario, most of the fishing supply stores have started stocking carp specific fishing tackle. The world of carp fishing with specialised equipment is far too vast and complex a subject for this local venue guide to take on. I will just cover the basics directly related to our starting locations. There are several online carp fishing suppliers located here in Ontario, and I highly recommend checking them out (see website address at end of book).

If you want to learn more about specific carp fishing techniques, with experienced fishermen who actively welcome newcomers, contact the Carp Anglers Group, they have a local chapter in Ontario.

You should also contact the Toronto Urban Fishing Ambassadors, right here in Toronto.

(See website addresses in the back of the book)

Due to the size of carp you will encounter, and their pulling power, carp rods are usually in the 12ft or 13ft range and capable of casting bait and weights in the 3 to 6 ounce range, for well over a hundred yards. Carp bait runner reels look similar to a large spinning reel, but usually come with a longer spool for low resistance distance casting, and a free clutch option to allow the carp to pick up the bait without feeling resistance.

Because traditional carp fishing involves fishing bait on the bottom at long distance, it's considered good practice to rest your rod in a horizontal position across rod supports. This allows for a smooth pick up by the fish, and facilitates the use of an electronic bite indicator on the line. You think you would notice the line moving without the bite indicator, but you won't. You'll miss that initial soft pick up unless you get a carp that takes the bait, and immediately runs with it. Invest in a decent landing net with a handle long enough to easily reach down into the water.

Carp

Sight fishing for carp in Toronto can be a simple affair that usually entails a single hair-rigged bait item, or a couple of corn kernels strung together on a hook, with maybe a few extra thrown into the water, next to the hook bait. Fishing at long distance at the outer harbour, or off the bays at TTP is far more effective when presenting larger bait offerings, spread accurately around the hair rigged hook bait.

Packbait

A popular local technique, based on the pay-lake carp fishing venues in the U.S, is the packbait presentation. You set up your hair rigged hook bait as normal and then pack your dampened particle bait tightly around the hook and compress it into a hard sausage or egg shape (mind that hook point in your hand!) The idea with the particle bait is to set off a drift of tiny particles and scents to draw the carp in. You want your particle bait to disperse a visible plume when it hits the water, with small particles flaking off it. Once it's on the bottom the main ball of bait slowly breaks apart, revealing your hook bait. You want enough small particles for the carp to pick at, while they zero in on your hook bait. Popular packbait ingredients are oats or polenta (grits).

Boilies

These are hard, round, carp specific baits, developed originally in the UK. You can purchase bags of Boilies at most fishing stores in the Toronto area. Boilies are very goby resistant due to their size, and available in a wide range of carp tested flavours. Boilies are easy to pierce and designed for threading onto a hair rig. They are also available as floating baits, allowing for a hair rig setup that is popped up, just off the bottom.

DIY

It's a pretty simple matter to make your own carp bait, either the U.K. boilie type or the North American catfish paste type. Recipes are outside the scope of this Toronto venue guide. If you run a quick web search for carp bait, you will find a wide range of recipes, to help you start with creating your own baits.

Toronto Salmon run

Chinook salmon

September usually kicks off the annual salmon run into the rivers across Toronto's waterfront. If you pick your spot and time, you can easily avoid the salmon insanity that occurs in hugely overcrowded locations, such as the Port Credit shoreline.

The best time of day by far is just before dawn. Next best is after sunset. It is possible to catch salmon in the river mouths during the main part of the day, but it is likely to be overcast or raining when you do.

The most common tactics are to use salmon eggs as bait, or to cast and retrieve spoons.

Eggs and roe bags

Salmon eggs can be fished static and weighted in place, or moving, bottom bounced or drifted under a float, in the current.

I use a modified drop shot rig for static fishing roe bags in current. In place of normal drop shot rig, attach a three way swivel onto your main line. Attach your weight on an 18" length of line to the bottom loop, and connect a 12" hook length to the centre loop of the three way swivel. Mount your roe bag onto the hook.

When you cast this out, the weight will hold position, and the roe bag will stand out from the main line on the hook length, moving around in the current. You can adapt the lengths of the lines, but always keep the hook leg shorter than the weight leg, so as to avoid tangles.

NOTE: You can buy salmon eggs from all the local fishing stores, either as tubs of singles or as ready-made "roe bags", tied in mesh. Please don't buy eggs illegally from another fisherman.

Spoons

The majority of my spoons are around four inches long. Light spoons provide the best flutter action at slower speeds, while Heavier, thicker spoons can be cast further, but need a faster retrieve rate. Spoons can be modified with glow tape, or you can purchase ready-made, glow in the dark spoons and spinners. You will need a flashlight to charge the glow tape on the spoon before casting it.

Mouth of the Humber

Mouth of the Humber River provides good salmon fishing in the early stages of the autumn run, as the salmon group up just offshore during the day. Very early mornings, and after sunset are best, either from the stone piers in the river mouth, or on the rocks outside of the white bridge (on either side of the river). Use spoons on the outside rocks, and roe bags in the river mouth current. Don't totally discount the main part of the day, especially if the day is overcast or there has been recent rain. Target the area directly under the white bridge, and also further upstream in the darkness around the supports beneath the road bridges.

Tommy Thompson Park

Weekend salmon fishing inside the East Cove and around the Lighthouse Point on Tommy Thompson Park can be extremely productive, if not one of the best spots downtown. As a bonus, the 5km walk each way usually keeps the location fairly quiet and peaceful. The deep, rocky nature of the cove leans towards the use of spoons rather than roe bags, unless you can find a decent spot near the gravel beach.

Toronto Island Pier

Toronto Island lookout pier is a prime overnight salmon fishing location when the run is on, but you will need a large drop net. If you don't have a net, but do have a decent beach casting rod, move north to the outside edge of Ward Island Beach. Both these locations allow you to target the shallows in front of the deep channel, just beyond the sand bar. The dredged channel runs up the length of the islands and turns into Eastern Gap. Both spoons and roe bags work well here.

Ward Island Beach

An excellent night fishing venue. Set up on the far outside edge of the beach, just inside the rock breakwall. Use roe bags at long distance.

Unwin Avenue

The Outer Harbour and Unwin Inlet areas also draw in stray salmon. I have caught a salmon from the gravel beach in front of the entrance to the Unwin Avenue inlet, while fishing at night with roe bags.

NOTE: It's not uncommon to see solitary salmon cruising around the Marinas, and the Ontario Place lagoons during the peak of the salmon run.

Rigs, worms and Cranks

Although we have two relatively short temperature zone windows for Bass around the Toronto Islands, it's worth understanding some of the more popular variations of presentations using plastic worms. I have listed the more common rigs that I have used in the weed beds and canals.

Texas Rigged Worm.

Texas rig

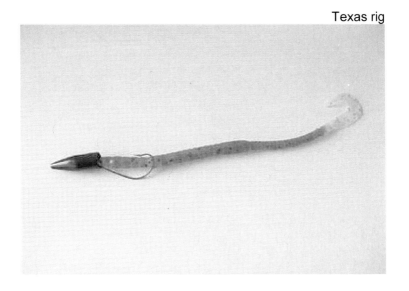

Thread a worm hook through the tip of the worm and twist the hook around, back into the worm, piercing the hook through the body.

The Texas rig is considered the go-to weedless setup for fishing plastic worm lures. To rig it weedless, rig the worm Texas style, and then put the point of the hook back under the surface of the worm. It will pop out with pressure from a fish bite, but won't snag into weeds as easily as an exposed hook point.

The weight in front of the hook is usually free running on the line. You can skip the lure across the bottom using a vertical twitch and release on retrieve. This will give the worm a nice injured up and down motion, with good variation in speed as the weight slides away from it on the drop and back to it on the upward retrieve. A small bead between the hook knot and the weight will add some sound when the bead and weight collide, and will also protect the knot from wear.

Generally, I only use this set up if the fish are actively biting. I'll switch to a slower presentation, such as a shaky head, or slack lining set up if the fish are being slow and lazy.

The Carolina Rig

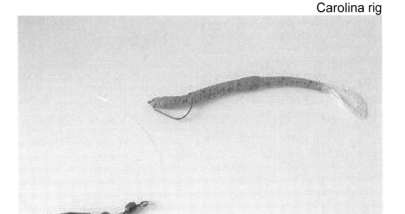

The main difference between a Carolina rig and a Texas rig is that on the Carolina rig the weight is usually set around 1 to 2ft in front of the hook on the other side of a swivel. The section of line between the weight and the worm allows the lure a wider range of free movement, during the drop and retrieve process.

The Carolina rig provides a number of options in presentations and their retrieving speeds. You can use the same vertical twitch and drop motion as with a Texas rigged worm, or you can slowly drag the weight across the bottom. If you are using a floating worm, the lure will stay swimming just above the bed.

Wacky Rigged Worm

Wacky rig

A wacky rigged worm is probably the simplest form of worm rig you will find. It's a drop rig, not designed to be drawn or played across the bottom in any way. This presentation is intended to be hit by fish on the slow fall before reaching bottom. Thicker, soft worms tend to perform best, the Senko worm is the go-to worm for most wacky rigs. The idea is for the worm to present a natural, undulating descent in front of the fish. You can use this for great results when plunking in thicker weeds beds, especially under overhanging tree cover.

If you are pitching and retrieving these worms some distance into heavy weeds, the hook can start to tear them up after a few casts. It is common practice to use a small piece of electrical tape or rubber tubing slipped over the worm and pierced by the hook, to give additional support.

Note: Ironically, trying to pull out the hook before you remove your protective tape or tubing will ensure that the hook barb does tear your worm up, so take the tape off first, before trying to replace the worm.

Shaky Head Rig

Shaky rig

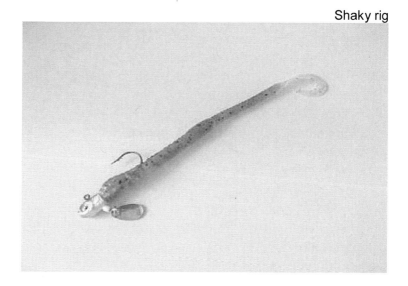

The shaky head rig is an excellent set up for slow days. This set up works best when slowly dragged and twitched across the bottom, or in combination with the slack lining technique. The shaky head rig is designed to be used with a floating worm, so that the tail sticks up and wiggles in the water. I use a horse head jig, as the additional blade really kicks up the dirt under the lure.

I prefer to use this presentation when fishing a sand or mud bottomed area. Not suitable for use among heavy weeds.

The Drop Shot rig

If you have young children and want to take them fishing along the Toronto waterfront, then you should consider putting together a simple drop shot fishing rig. The drop-shot method is considered a "finesse bass fishing technique", which sounds all fancy and expert level, but in reality it's just another variation of a Paternoster rig, one of the oldest fishing setups in existence, and about as simple a fishing technique for kids, as you can find.

The drop shot rig, as the name implies, was originally designed for dropping straight down over the side of a boat. But for urban fishing in Toronto, it's also perfect for dropping straight down a few feet out from the harbour or canal wall, dangling over the side of a bridge or pitching into a gap in a patch of weeds next to the shoreline. With pan fish in abundance across the Toronto Waterfront, summer is a great time of year for this style of fishing, and there's no overhead casting involved so it's a safer way to get younger kids started.

Drop Shot fishing rig: The Basics

You have your fishing weight at the very end of your line, and for pan fishing with the kids, your hook sticks out on the fishing line approximately 6 to12 inches above it, and that's it.

Once you have dropped your line in, you let it sink, but only until you can feel the weight just touching the bottom. This keeps the tension on your line, and has the hook sticking out at 90 degrees. When the kids get a bite from a fish, they feel it immediately pulling down on the rod, as the weight is the other side of the hook, not between them and the fish.

Drop shot rig

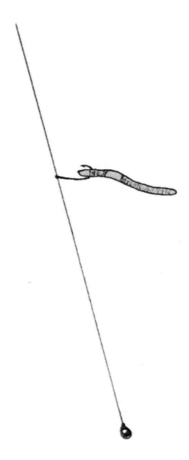

Yes… it is difficult to get overly technical about describing the drop shot fishing setup, but I do have a few useful tips for you.

Split shot weights

Reusable lead-free split shot weights – Instead of buying leaded fishing weights, purchase one or two bags of the larger sized, re-usable split shot weights, somewhere around $1.50 to $2 for a bag of about twenty. Please buy the lead free type, it's worth it in the long run.

Split shot weights

Squeeze three or four of your split shot close together onto the very end of your line. You will get fewer underwater snags than with a larger, single weight (which costs more money too) and if you do get snagged on something, the fishing line can be easily pulled through the split shot saving the hook, and you can quickly squeeze on a few replacement split shot and carry on.

Standoff Hooks

While you can use pretty much any hook for your drop shot rig, there actually is a hook specifically designed for this kind of set up.

Standoff hook

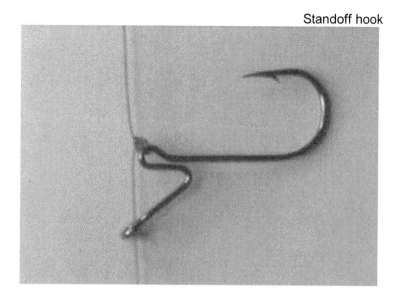

The standoff hook ties on at the bend in the hook and the fishing line then passes down through the eye of the hook, on its way to the weight. This causes the hook to stand out straight from the fishing line. Whichever type of hook you go with, it needs to be tied on with the point facing upwards, with the line tailing off below it. Your weight(s) go onto the very end of the trailing line.

Drop shot Bait

The Common Earthworm is a great choice for pan fish, bass, perch and pretty much most other fish species. If you have a garden with a lawn, you can probably collect your own fresh worms. You will need a couple of buckets of water, a flashlight and a lidded container to put the worms in. Go out to your lawn well after dark, pour the water onto a small area about 3ft by 3ft, thoroughly soaking it and wait 10 minutes. Any worms under the lawn will surface to avoid drowning (oh, the irony!), quickly pick them up and place them into your container. Once you have enough, add some loose dirt or some damp shredded newspaper to the container. Don't forget that worms need air! Remember to make some holes in the lid of your container before putting the worms in the fridge, ready to go fishing the next day.

If you don't have access to a garden space, you can purchase live worms at most fishing stores. Small Minnows also make a great drop shot bait. Use the preserved ones that come in a jar at the fishing store, they last a lot longer and are more cost effective.

Using live fish as bait can be very complicated under the local fishing regulations, especially if they didn't come from the area you are fishing in. (a BIG no-no).

Lures

Soft plastic fishing lures with the curly tails that wiggle with any water motion, such as the "Mister Twister" range are an excellent option for the drop shot set up in moving water. They last a long time, they are easy to store and cheap to buy, you can usually pick up a pack of small ones for a few dollars online, or at your local fishing store and you just hook one on.

Micro lures

Younger kids don't care how big or small the fish is, as long as they catch a few. Get some cheap micro lures for around $3 for five, including two micro jig heads. When you run out of the little plastic worm tails, wrap a small thin piece of shiny aluminum foil onto the back of the micro jig head instead.

Double Dip

I have had good success using a double rig version of the drop shot where I replace the end of line split shots, with a skirted jig head. On a mud or silt bottom the movement of the skirted jig usually kicks up enough particles to bring the fish in to investigate.

If the water you are fishing has no movement, you can give the occasional little twitch, but most people tend to overdo this. You want the suspended lure to wiggle naturally, not leap around in a threatening manner.

As crankbaits are so effective in catching so many of the species we can target locally, I thought that a quick review on the basics of crankbaits, and how to tell a shallow running crank lip from a deep diver, might be useful.

The first thing to get out of the way when discussing lipped crankbaits is the lipless crankbaits. Lipless cranks are mostly* sinking lures, unlike the various lipped crankbaits which are mostly* floating or neutral buoyancy, and use the lip in order to dive.

*Yes there are many exceptions to this generalisation, some of which I mention at the end of the article, but for the purpose of understanding the basics we will be applying this over-simplified generalization.

Lipless crankbaits use their flat-sided body design and the high position of the top-mounted line tie to produce a narrow swimming action.

I think it's worth pointing out that the swimming action of the lipless crankbait is intentionally designed as a far more subtle vibrating action, than the typical wide wobble action of a lipped crankbait. So, don't throw out those lipless cranks because they appear to have no action, they're actually working just fine.

The tight vibrating action of a good quality lipless crankbait produces high-frequency vibrations that mimic a wounded baitfish. Generally speaking, because a lipless crank doesn't have the drag caused by a diving lip it is possible to retrieve it at extremely fast speeds, and the faster you retrieve the more intense the vibrations. On the flip side, lipless cranks tend to be poor performers at very slow speeds, especially when compared to a jointed, lipped crankbait.

Lipless, sinking crankbaits will immediately drop through the water column when you cast them out, making these lures useful for targeting fish that are suspended mid or deep water. They generally drop at a rate of a foot a second, allowing you to count them down to a specific depth. The expensive ones come with the sink rate printed on the box. There are a few factors however, that can alter the sink rate, such as your fishing line and water currents. It's always worth applying your own '1 Mississippi, 2 Mississippi' sink rate count test on any new lipless cranks, so you know how fast the crank sinks, at your normal rate of counting.

The basics

The length and angle of a crankbait lip determines if it's a deep, shallow, or medium diver. The width of the lip blade compared to the width of the main body, determines the side to side motion....That's it, the end. OK. Not really the end, but understanding how the lip effects action, doesn't have to be any more complicated than that.

Buoyancy

The majority of today's mass produced crankbaits contain air chambers that house small metal Ball Bearings. These Ball Bearings emit sound and vibrations when the crankbait moves through the water, which hopefully alerts any nearby predator fish. Without getting overly technical, the size and position of the hollow chamber dictates the buoyancy of the crankbait and determines whether it's a surface floater or suspends in the water when you stop retrieving.

Crankbaits labeled as floating will slowly rise to the surface if you stop retrieving them. When you restart the retrieve, the crankbait will dive according to the angle of the lip. Floating crankbaits are usually the best choice for fishing shallow waters, or water that has heavy weed growth. Floating crankbaits tend to move forward with a head down angle. This puts the lip out front and protects the belly hook behind it. These lures also have a tendency to float up backwards, useful for backing it up from obstacles when you pause the retrieve, or relax the line.

Suspending baits will float on the surface, dive down on the retrieve but will hover and maintain a constant depth when the reeling of the line is halted. This style of bait is great for targeting fish that follow and attack on the pause, or for fish that hunt at a specific depth. Smallmouth, pike and walleye are prime targets for suspended crankbaits.

Lip size and angle

Longer, narrower lips that are connected straight out forward from the nose of the crankbait will dive the deepest, and have the tightest side to side motion. Wide lips that are connected at 60 to 90 degrees down from the front of the crankbait will run shallowest, and have a wide side motion. Lips that are positioned at 30 to 45 degrees will have medium wiggle and medium diving depth.

Shallow running crankbait

A shallow diving crankbait possesses the smallest lip and the steepest angle. It will generally dive less than 5 feet and is used for very shallow water or skimming over the tops of tall weeds.

Medium running crankbait

The medium diver has a slightly larger, narrower lip at an angle of around 30 to 45 degrees and can run at depths between 5 and 12 feet.

A deep diving lure has a large lip positioned at a flat angle; some lips are almost as long as the lures body itself. These deep runners can go down more than twenty feet.

Line Tie Position

The position of the connection point between the line and the crankbait affects a crankbait's action and diving depth. Take a second look at the shallow running crankbait picture, and you will see that the line connection point is not even on the lip, it's on the front of the head. Now take a second look at the deep running crankbait picture. The line tie on point is halfway down the lip.

Hook Size

It's common practice when buying cheap, mass produced cranks to upgrade the rings and hooks. If you go this route, keep in mind that the hook size directly affects the crankbaits motion and buoyancy. The hooks act in a similar manner to a boat keel by providing downward stability to the lure. Generally speaking, larger hooks offer more stability. However, if the hook is too large, it will also be too heavy, and negatively affect the lure's action, by transforming from keel to anchor. Ideally you want a hook just large enough to provide stability and cleanly hook into your target fish, but small enough to minimize any anchor effect.

The effect of the hook's weight on the lure increases as the distance between it and the line tie increases, meaning that hooks at the rear of the bait will have a greater effect on the lure's swimming action than hooks at the front. Be wary of swapping out a rear treble for a large single hook that has an offset to its curve as this can cause the crankbait to no longer run true in the water.

If you want to change your hook, go ahead, but be prepared to go out and experiment with the modified crankbait in clear water, so you can see what unintentional action changes you may have made.

Crankbait Body Size

These are the suggested species-specific crankbait sizes:

Crappie 1-3 inches
Bass 2-5 inches
Northern Pike 4-9 inches

I will admit that except when I am targeting pike, I tend to run my crankbaits on the smaller end of suggested size scale as I have had most success with micro lure sized baits, attracting more species of fish....

Mini-Cranks

Exceptions to my scandalous floaters and sinkers generalization....

The Minnow Crankbait

Minnow Crankbait

The minnow crankbait has undergone significant development in recent years, and you can now find a minnow style crankbait of whatever performance type you require. They can be cranked, popped, trolled, fished top-water as floaters, or paused mid-water at a depth of your choosing.

The Minnow crank typically has a long slender profile, a small shallow diving lip, and slow keel side to side rolling action. At one time the diving lip was always a shallow diving lip, but recently manufacturers have begun offering deeper running models. The longer, slim profile doesn't offer the belly hook protection you get from a head down wide body crank, so you need to keep more of an eye out for snagging. Many manufacturers now also offer floating, slow-rising, and suspending versions.

The suspending models perform in a similar fashion to suspended wide body cranks, resting at a specific depth and allowing you to pause and 'hover" the crank directly over fish holding cover.

Jointed Cranks

The jointed crankbait consists of two or more hinged body segments that create an exaggerated wiggle, even at slow retrieval speeds, giving the appearance of an erratic moving bait fish, unable to gain speed.

Fishing for pike after the season re-opens and they are well rested from spawning, I tend to favour a jointed body crankbait over the straight body types. I think the jointed crankbait has features that are giving me some additional advantages, namely more movement and vibration noise at much slower retrieval speeds when compared to the single piece crankbaits.

Early season pike fishing in the Toronto area usually means low weed cover, so I am fishing hard structure such as the corners of harbour walls. Cold water visibility can also be good during the day so a jointed crankbait with good wiggle motion will give both decent rattle and flash as it moves along, even at a dead slow speed.

When I rig a jointed crankbait I prefer to use a wide loop knot on the front and ensure that the crankbait is completely free on the loop to give the maximum side to side motion that it has to offer. Very little forward movement is then required to get a decent side to side wobble going.

The illusion of speed and distress.

Because jointed crankbaits wobble so well even at slow speed retrieval they look like they're trying to move quickly away, but just can't. Perfect for fooling your target into thinking that your lure is an easy meal, an injured baitfish trying to move out of range, and enticing a strike and hook up. I can't overstress the importance of getting a decent jointed crankbait for hi-movement, slow speed retrieval work.

Summer weeds

Come the summer in Toronto and I tend to be a lot more reserved on using my jointed crankbaits. The wider side to side slashing action of the jointed crank tail section gets caught up in summertime's heavy weed growth far more readily than the single bodied cranks, and I can spend a lot more time weed pulling along the Harbourfront than fishing. Early and late season tends to be the time of year that I reach for the jointed lures first.

Exception: Fishing from the Toronto Islands lookout pier onto the sand flats behind the Islands, allows for the use of jointed cranks year round, without fear of snags. They have proven very effective at night from the pier. The additional sound generated from the joint sections will attract fish from across the flats. Jointed cranks have also been useful in heavily stained water, such as the river mouths when the fall rains are flooding. I have modified a few of my jointed cranks with glow dots and dressed tail hooks for salmon fishing.

Useful Websites

Ministry of Natural Resources
http://www.mnr.gov.on.ca/en/
Check the fishing sub-site for current regulations, and license details.

Toronto Urban Fishing Ambassadors
http://torontourbanfishing.com/
Local fishing group that provides front line support for fishing events.

Ontario Shore Fishing Forum
http://ontarioshorefishing.com/forum/
A friendly, open fishing forum, specialising in shore fishing around the Toronto area.

Ontario Carp Anglers Group
http://www.carpanglersgroup.com/forum/index.php?/forum/120-ontario/
This group welcomes new carp fisherman and can help get you started on carp specific techniques.

Toronto Islands Ferry service:
http://www.torontoislandferryfinder.com/
Tickets and schedules

TTC: http://www.ttc.ca/index.jsp
Toronto's public transport system. Grab a system map, so that you can reach the fishing locations via public transport.

Bass Pro, Vaughn: http://www.basspro.com/
Bass Pro has a superstore at Vaughn Mills mall.

Sail, Etobicoke: http://www.sail.ca/en/home/
Sail has a store close to Sherway Gardens.

LeBarons: http://www.lebaron.ca/index_en.html
There's a lebarons store located on Dundas East in Mississauga. (A good place for salmon eggs and ready-made roe bags.)

New World Carp: http://newworldcarp.com/osc/
Online Carp specific tackle and bait store. Located in Ontario, low cost shipping.

West Marine: http://www.westmarine.com/
Located at lakeshore and lower Jarvis. Mainly boat supplies, but the store does have an aisle of rods, reels, and lures.

Throughout my adult life I am lucky enough to have travelled extensively for work purposes, and I have become expert in finding the space to pack a good quality travel rod into my bag. Among the highlights on my travels, I have fished for big Stripers in the Colorado River below the Hoover Dam, jigged for Cod from the side of a lifeboat at Svalbard, and learned how to balloon fish the reef, local style in Aruba.

I first came to Canada in 1999, and I lived in Halifax, Nova Scotia, where I spent my spare time fishing for Mackerel and Cod. When the opportunity arose, I moved out west to Alberta, and made the most of the short summer fishing season for big Lake Trout in Banff national park, before learning to ice fish on Spray Lakes in Canmore.

I moved to Toronto in 2004, and since then I have fished on a regular basis for pike, bass, carp, salmon and perch along the Toronto shoreline and city parks, using lures for open water and drop shot rigs during the high weeds of summer.

If you see me fishing somewhere on the waterfront, stop and say hello, I am always happy to chat about the awesome fishing in Toronto.

Mike Harry